MOVE US 2 PANAMA

Aaron D. Smith

Disclaimer

The information provided in this book is intended for general informational purposes only. It is not intended as legal, financial, or professional advice and should not be considered as such.

The author and publisher have made every effort to ensure the accuracy and completeness of the content within this book at the time of publication. However, laws, regulations, and circumstances may change over time, and the information contained herein may become outdated or no longer applicable.

Before making any decisions related to relocating from the United States to Panama, it is strongly recommended that readers consult with relevant experts, authorities, and professionals to obtain up-to-date and tailored advice specific to their individual circumstances.

The author and publisher disclaim any liability, loss, or risk incurred as a consequence, directly or indirectly, of the use and application of the information provided in this book. Readers are urged to exercise due diligence and seek professional guidance as necessary when considering such a significant life change.

Relocating to a foreign country involves complex legal, financial, and personal decisions, and this book should serve as a starting point for your research and decision-making process rather than a definitive guide.

CONTENTS

Introduction

In 2023, a season of change swept over my family. My wife Dara, our two sons, and I were going separate ways as our now adult children spread their wings and flew from our nest in Central Texas. Everyone hopes to see their children grow up and live their lives, but in doing so, my wife and I had a home that suddenly felt too expansive for just the two of us. Coupled with this were dwindling professional opportunities as we approached our mature years. And if we are speaking honestly, we felt a growing sense of pessimism in our lifestyle and financial future in the United States. Growing political polarization, increased access to guns and gun violence, and other factors caused us to have very matter-of-fact discussions on our future in Texas.

Like so many others in similar situations, we set our sights on charting a course for the next chapter of our journey. We weren't quite ready for the traditional notion of retirement, but we were eager for new adventures. Our vision? A tropical haven, not too far away, equipped with modern infrastructure and accessible routes back to the U.S. to be close to family when needed. This marked the commencement of our relocation journey to Panama.

If you've picked up this workbook, chances are, you too, are standing at the crossroads of transition. Perhaps you've entertained the idea of life beyond familiar shores and yearn for insights from someone who's taken that leap. Consider this workbook a heartfelt offering from me to you. My mission? To guide and prepare you for your transition from the United States. Within these pages, you'll meticulously map out your plan, identify essential documents, and set the stage for your Panamanian attorney to facilitate your move.

Are you ready to embark on this exciting journey? Let's dive in...

The Timeline

The most important aspect of planning your exit, aside from ensuring you have the money, is establishing a timeline. The timeline is based on your goals, your partner's goals, and anyone dependent on you.

When my wife and I decided to move to Panama in 2022, we set the goal of 2024 for the move. We had a college senior and freshman financially dependent on us. We had a house with 25 years of collected memories stored in every closet, garage, and rafter and tucked into drawers. We had time-bound benefits tied to our employer – requiring that we stay at least through 2023 or risk leaving "money on the table."

If you are not yet of retirement age to withdraw from a pension or social security, you already know that you should have a sizable nest egg set aside. Even with that, you should still consider and inventory your skills and experiences that may lead you to a new career or business opportunity. I'm not a financial planner, and the goal of this workbook is not to provide guidance other than recommending that you have a plan to address how you will fund the next years until you reach retirement age when other benefits will kick in.

When moving to Panama, it is important to remember there are effectively four visa options to choose from aside from the tourist visa useful for short exploratory trips:

1. Friendly Nations Visa, which allows up to 90 days stay in Panama.

2. Pensionado Visa or the retirement visa.

3. Short Stay Visa, also known as the Digital Nomad Visa

4. Qualified Investor Visa, also known as the Golden Visa.

Yes, other visa options are available, but for many expats, these are used. You can find the complete list on the Panama Consulate website. Each of these visa options has different requirements to meet. For example, the qualified investor is a program that can streamline gaining residency in Panama. But with it comes different qualifications and expenses than the others. Consider your strategic goals and the counsel of those who have come before you when making your plan.

After factoring in your personal financial situation and the time it will take to downsize from your current residence, establish your goal for your move. This is probably a good time to inform you that Panama, unlike the United States, loves its holidays and time off. It will be very difficult (not impossible) to complete a move in November or December and probably even January, so be sure to factor this into your plans.

Write your goal date here:

With your relocation date established, we can work backward and ensure you have everything you need to complete your new mission! And don't worry if the date changes. It's meant to be a target to keep your activities progressing. Other tasks that come below may accelerate your timeframe or postpone it. Either way, it's going to be okay.

Now, let's go into the details....

Friendly Nations Visa (Visa de Países Amigos)

This visa was designed to attract citizens from certain countries that maintain friendly relations with Panama, making it easier for them to obtain residency and work in the country. The United States was among the countries included in the program.

The requirements for the Friendly Nations Visa, as of 2021, were:

1. **Proof of nationality:** The primary applicant must be a citizen of one of the countries considered "friendly" to Panama. The USA is listed, and the complete list is published here: https://www.embassyofpanama.org/visas-1

2. **Economic solvency:** The main applicant needed to prove economic solvency. This was typically done by:

- Opening a bank account in Panama with a minimum balance of USD $5,000 (and an additional $2,000 for each dependent).

- Economic or professional ties to Panama: This could be proven by either setting up a Panamanian company or by getting a job in Panama.

3. **Passport:** A valid passport and a second form of photo ID from the applicant's country of origin.

4. **Five passport-sized photos.**

5. **Criminal background check:** From the applicant's country of origin or place of residence for the past two years. The report must be authenticated by the Panamanian consulate or apostilled.

6. **Health certificate:** Issued by a licensed Panamanian doctor.

7. **Dependents:** If the main applicant wants to bring dependents, additional documentation (like marriage and birth certificates) is needed. These documents typically needed to be apostilled or authenticated by the Panamanian consulate.

As a result of the requirements above, this visa is especially popular among certain types of American expats. These include the following:

1. **Young families:** Some young American families seek a different, perhaps more affordable, lifestyle or want to give their children a bi-cultural upbringing.

2. **Investors and Entrepreneurs:** Those looking to start businesses in Panama or invest in Panamanian ventures often use this visa as an entry point.

The Pensionado Visa, AKA Retirement Visa

Panama's "Pensionado Visa" (or Retiree Visa) is one of the most popular residency programs for retirees globally, largely due to the benefits it offers and the country's attractive living conditions. When you are granted a Pensionado Visa, you are effectively given Jubilado status benefits. I mention it here because many times I have seen Pensionado and Jubilado interchanged. But as you will see, the Jubilado has an age requirement (55 for female and 60 for male) which the Pensionado Visa does not have. In any case, any visa can be combined with Jubilado once the age requirements are met.

Panama Pensionado Visa Requirements:

1. **Proof of Pension:** The applicant must provide proof of a lifetime pension or retirement income. As of 2021, the minimum amount required is USD $1,000 per month. If you buy real estate valued at USD $100,000 or more, this monthly requirement drops to $750.

2. **No Minimum Age:** While this visa targets retirees, there's technically no age limit. If someone younger can demonstrate the required pension or retirement income, they can qualify.

3. **Valid Passport:** A passport that remains valid for at least another six months from the application date.

4. **Health Certificate:** Obtained from a Panamanian doctor.

5. **Background Check:** A criminal background check from the applicant's home country or place of residence for the past two years. The report needs to be apostilled or authenticated by a Panamanian consulate.

6. **Dependents:** Dependents can be included, but the primary applicant will need to demonstrate an additional $250 per month in pension income for each dependent.

Benefits:

1. **Tax Breaks:** Exemption from taxes on any foreign-earned income.

2. **Discounts:** Various discounts, including:

- 50% off entertainment (movies, theater, concerts, etc.)

- 30% off bus, boat, and train fares

- 25% off airline tickets

- 25% off monthly energy bills applies if you are the subscriber, not the landlord.

- 30% to 50% off hotel stays, depending on the day of the week.

- 20% off medical consultations

- 15% off hospital bills (if no insurance applies)

- 10% off prescription medicines

3. **One-Time Import Tax Exemption:** For household goods up to a total of $10,000.

4. **Tax Exemption:** Every two years on the importation of a car.

While this visa appears to have similarities with the friendly nations visa, they have some differences.

Differences between a Pensionado Visa and a Friendly Nations Visa:

1. **Purpose:** The Pensionado Visa is specifically designed for retirees, while the Friendly Nations Visa is broader, targeting citizens of specific countries (like the U.S.) who want to live, work, or start a business in Panama.

2. **Income Source:** Pensionado applicants must prove a permanent pension income, while Friendly Nations Visa applicants

need to demonstrate economic solvency, often via a Panamanian bank deposit or by establishing economic ties (like starting a company).

3. **Benefits:** The Pensionado Visa offers specific discounts and tax breaks tailored to retirees, while the Friendly Nations Visa does not.

Typical Profile of an American Expat Using the Pensionado Visa:

1. **Retirees (general):** Individuals who've retired from their careers and receive a consistent pension or retirement income.

2. **Retirees Seeking a Lower Cost of Living:** Those looking to stretch their retirement dollars in a country with a lower cost of living compared to the U.S.

3. **Retirees Seeking Lifestyle Change:** Individuals or couples wanting a change of scenery, climate, or culture.

4. **Retirees Seeking Tax Benefits:** Those wanting to benefit from Panama's favorable tax policies, especially on foreign-earned income.

5. **Retirees Seeking Medical Access:** Retirees attracted to Panama's growing medical tourism industry and quality healthcare at a fraction of U.S. costs.

In essence, while both the Pensionado and Friendly Nations Visas offer pathways to Panamanian residency, they cater to different audiences and come with distinct requirements and benefits. Always consult with a local Panamanian attorney or expert for the most updated and accurate information.

The Short Stay Visa, AKA Digital Nomad Visa

In May 2021, Panama updated a new "Short Stay Visa as a Remote Worker" within the non-resident immigration category. This visa aims to make Panama an attractive destination for remote workers, leveraging the changing global work trends accelerated by the COVID-19 pandemic. This initiative is expected to boost the Panamanian economy through increased investment and consumption of local goods and services.

Benefits of the Visa:

- The visa allows foreign remote workers to live and work in Panama without requiring additional permissions from any other governmental department.

Eligibility Requirements:

1. The applicant must have an employment contract with a foreign company or be self-employed, specifically in a teleworking (remote work) capacity.

2. The work performed must primarily affect regions/countries outside of Panama.

3. The individual must earn an income from a foreign source, with a yearly total of at least thirty-six thousand balboas (B/36,000.00) or its equivalent in another currency ($36,000 USD).

This visa is especially popular among Digital Nomads and Remote Workers. Given the relatively low cost of living and the ability to start a company in Panama, digital nomads, and remote workers may find this visa appealing.

The Qualified Investor, AKA Golden Visa

Panama introduced the "Qualified Investor Visa" as a means to attract high-net-worth individuals and stimulate foreign investment in the country. This visa is aimed primarily at those willing to make substantial investments in Panama, and it provides a pathway to permanent residency in a comparatively short timeframe, oftentimes in as little as a couple of months.

Requirements for the Qualified Investor Visa:

1. **Investment Options:** The main applicant must make a substantial investment in Panama through one of the following avenues:

- Investment in real estate with a minimum value of USD $300,000. This amount will likely increase to USD $500,000 as the popularity of the program has proven itself in the first years following the pandemic.

- Investment in a fixed-term deposit in a Panamanian bank for a minimum amount of USD $300,000.

- Investment in a recognized Panamanian business for a minimum amount of USD $500,000.

2. **Validity:** The visa is granted provisionally for two years before being made permanent. You will have permanent residency as long as you maintain the investment option for the required period. Check with your attorney for specifics.

3. **Due Diligence:** A due diligence background check will be conducted on the main applicant and any dependents over 18 years of age.

4. **Passport:** A valid passport and possibly other forms of identification from the applicant's country of origin.

5. **Six passport-sized photos.**

6. **Criminal Background Check:** From the applicant's country of origin or the country where they've lived for the past two years. The report must be apostilled.

7. **Dependents:** The main applicant can include dependents in the application, and the necessary documentation (like marriage and birth certificates) will be required. These documents will need to be apostilled or authenticated by the Panamanian consulate.

The types of American expats who may find the Qualified Investor Visa as their best option:

1. **High-Net-Worth Individuals**: Those who have the financial means to make substantial investments and are seeking an expedited pathway to permanent residency in Panama.

2. **Real Estate Investors:** Individuals looking to invest significantly in Panamanian real estate, either for personal use, rental income, or speculation. Important to note, this is generally assumed to be a cash purchase. Financing a real estate purchase may not qualify for this visa.

3. **Business Entrepreneurs:** Those looking to establish a substantial business presence in Panama or invest in existing businesses.

4. **Retirees with High Assets:** Retirees who have accumulated significant assets and want to diversify their investments while gaining residency in a tropical country.

5. **Family Relocation:** Families who wish to relocate to Panama and have the means to make a substantial investment. This

can be motivated by a desire for a different lifestyle, business opportunities, or other personal reasons.

The Qualified Investor Visa can be particularly appealing because of the expedited pathway to permanent residency. However, as always, potential applicants should consult with a knowledgeable immigration attorney in Panama to understand the most up-to-date requirements and the pros and cons of this visa option versus others.

As the name implies, a requirement of the qualified investor is financial investment in the country. Usually, this comes in the form of real estate purchases, but not exclusively. You could choose to move your money to a Panama bank as a means of diversification. While this seems straightforward, trust me when I tell you that it is not.

This has been an overview of the visa types, benefits, and who uses them. As someone who has relocated to Panama City, most new expats that I have met are retired and receiving a pension. Usually, that pension is from the military, which means the retirees themselves are somewhat younger than you might expect. This does not mean the environment is necessarily pro-military. Many have left those days far in the past and are set on defining their new lifestyle. They are in the process of the Pensionado and have a temporary cedula in possession. However, there are lifestyle differences that come with being a retired person on a Pensionado as compared with someone using a golden visa. There are also limitations as to what you can do in Panama if on a Pensionado visa compared to a qualified investor's golden visa.

Write your attorney firm here:

Name:

Address:

Cell/WhatsApp:

Backup attorney:

Write the Visa program that you are pursuing here:

Write the expected date you will receive your visa:

Congratulations on your progress! You've identified your timeframe, your visa requirements, and your attorney. The next pages will delve into the details of the requirements. Your attorney will ask that you provide the necessary documents, but if they have never lived in the USA, they might be unfamiliar with the process of getting the documents in the correct format. The majority of this workbook is dedicated to helping you, your lawyer, and any other party you work with to have a smooth process with reasonable expectations.

Banking in Panama

When you open a bank account with a mega bank in the United States, you may consider Chase, Morgan Stanley, Wells Fargo, and Schwab, among others. Maybe you are loyal to a community credit union. You might even have a banking service that isn't a traditional bank: Bluevine, Chime, and Wise are often used. We use both Schwab and Morgan Stanley international banking. These accounts are good to have as a first step in your move to become an expat.

Why?

Because they may offer a waiver of international transaction fees and may make it easier for you to make an international wire transfer – something you will value when it's time to fund your new Panama bank account.

Does your bank have a branch in Panama? It can be confusing, so take note: even if your bank has international banking as a benefit, you will eventually need an account in Panama. Even though your bank may have commercial banking centers in Panama City, it may not provide personal banking services. What then are your choices? I've found that most people and small businesses use a Panama local bank. These include:

- Banco General (if you intend to make payments digitally in Panama, the app Yappy is owned by Banco General)

- Banistmo

- BAC International

- Others

Other international banks:

- BBVA Panama

- Scotiabank

- Banco Lafise

- Others

To get a bank account is an exercise in patience. Some banks will not consider opening an account for American's who are not in the visa process. Even then, I've heard of it taking from one to three hours to open an account. If you were ever wondering about bank safety, don't. The banking system is secure, based on the compliance requirements that are in place and the physical security of armed guards positioned at the entrance. Don't worry, they are friendly, and the bank is safe.

Selecting your bank is a personal decision. Many of the same factors used to decide your current bank might factor into your decision. What are the interest rates? What fees are they charging?

Can you develop a personal relationship with your banker? This is why the bank we selected will be different from the one you choose. Your attorney should introduce you to several banks to help you make the decision. Ask the prospective banks to schedule a Zoom call, and most will happily agree. It also provides them the opportunity to ensure an English speaker is available to talk with you.

What will you need to open an account?

The following is my list for Scotiabank, which we chose based on our interactions with the branch general manager. Lucas is bilingual and very specific and deliberate with his words. From our earliest interactions, it was clear to me he had our best interest. This is how we engaged with him early on:

- Introduction from Panama attorney

- Valid ID (Passport)

- Second ID (Driver's License or Migration Card)

- Proof of Income (Your Retiree Certificate or Tax Returns)

- Complete and sign bank documents

- Six months of account movement or Bank Reference Letter

We met with Scotiabank via Zoom meeting and were pleased with the services they provide. We then sent our documents and scheduled an in-person meeting to complete the accounts setup. Yes, it is important to consider that opening a bank account will likely require you to be physically in the country. Most will not consider opening an account for non-residents. But they will not say this to you. They will simply ignore your emails and phone calls.

To be clear, business does not move at the pace you may be accustomed to. But there is a difference between delays and being blown off. You will know when the line has been crossed. These documents should be assembled prior to meeting with your selected bank. Providing them digitally in advance (email) will make the process go that much faster.

Signatures for official documents:

As you begin your new life as an expat, be sure that you are consistently signing documents as your signature appears on your passport. I have a habit of signing using my middle initial only, but when I see a document with my full first name, middle name, and last name, I sign using my full name. This error resulted in me having to DHL correctly signed documents to my new bank at an expensive amount.

Downsizing and Moving Companies

It may be obvious already, but if it hasn't yet hit you – you have a lot of stuff. You need a plan for what to do with it. Can you sell it? Do you donate it? What should you keep?

While I can't make those decisions for you, I can make some recommendations on how to decide and what you should consider.

There will be items that you have kept that have sentimental value. Maybe they have been in your family for generations, and you want to hand them to your children and your children's children. It's time to have that conversation. When we assessed some of the items, we were very worried about how to store them. After a conversation with both sons and even extended family members, we learned that none had ever wanted them! This made it easy to decide what went to consignment. Other items were delivered to them or sent to the family with clear instructions on who they belonged to. It's also a good idea to update your will accordingly.

What to keep with you really depends on how you believe your lifestyle will settle. We decided many of our clothes, mostly winter, were not going to make the journey to our new year-round tropical environment. Those garments we chose to keep for our winter trips to New York and Colorado, we vacuum sealed.

Dara, my wife, is all about her Peloton. You can follow her on *Lovetruth12*. When we decided to move, I knew she would not let go of her treadmill or bike. What Peloton has created in its community is truly remarkable from a marketing perspective. I've wondered who might acquire them in the months following the end of the pandemic. Honestly, I thought Meta was the most likely to acquire them for both the community and the potential hardware tie-in.

Moving exercise equipment like this is more than I can put onto a flight. This is where an international moving company like Canal Movers was exactly what we needed. There are other moving companies for sure. Our experience with Canal Movers is based on the prices, the experiences with the sub-contractors who estimated our move and loaded our belongings onto a truck, and the flexibility of the final delivery.

Also, your belongings could arrive in Panama before you are ready. Be prepared to connect your attorney to your mover to ensure the paperwork necessary for clearing customs is available and doesn't create additional headaches.

When we moved, we appreciated that Canal Movers would hold our belongings for a small fee as we completed the process to make our apartment move-in ready with paint, furniture, and appliances.

Buying a House or Apartment

Have you seen the skyline? Of course you have! Or maybe you spent time at the beach. You want to move here. While the community around you might advocate that you rent, there are other reasons that you might want to purchase. This was me.

When I came to visit in 2022, the real estate market in Texas was still soaring. When we came home and began our inventory of items to take and items to leave behind, there were some big-ticket items that I didn't want to move more than once for fear of damage. When I did my financial models, even overpaying a little was still advantageous to rent in perpetuity. I knew once we committed to our "retirement" to Panama, there was no returning to the USA for anything other than a visit. The politics, the people, the weather. My family was ready for a change of scenery and culture.

But you learn. We found an apartment in an area we loved: it had a park right outside our door for dog walks. It was near two supermercados. While not on Avenida Balboa, it was very convenient to the Cinta Costera for morning exercise. We were told that the market was a bit soft, and we could negotiate the price. This turned out not to be not entirely true.

In real estate, we are taught in the USA not to fall in love with any one property. You lose leverage. However, if you have very specific requirements, you do have a scarcity of options. The building that we chose was sold out of units, and the owner of ours was an investor, ready to hold out as long as necessary for his price.

Then came the buying process that was foreign to us. It wasn't that lawyers ran the process; it was that sometimes, it seemed we were training our attorney to get the process moving. For example, when you find an apartment, you work with your agent first on a verbal offer. Then, the lawyers take over to write the contract. We had already returned to Texas by the time the formal offer was made and were in New York City when we learned the apartment was still on the market. Until our offer was signed and the 10% down payment to the seller (not escrow), the seller was not obligated to hold for us. Why should he? So, we searched for a way to have a signed offer presented. DocuSign, long used by real estate agents in the US, does not stand up in courts in Panama. The solution? Giving the attorney a limited power of attorney (PoA) for the real estate transaction.

Giving PoA is not a big deal and should not have concerned us and would have saved us both time and an 'emergency' return flight to Panama to sign the documents. The seller agreed to take a 10% payment via international wire transfer (FYI – read the banking section). But to make the final payment would require a certified check from a Panama-based bank.

Back at home, we had put our house on the market, and our belongings were now in transit to the Panama Canal via LCL shipment. The shipper was able to take our items because our well-respected attorney committed that, pending the purchase of the apartment, we would be in the process for the Golden Visa.

In retrospect, I would advise most to heed the warnings of those who have come before. Rent for a while. We love the apartment we chose, and anyone we have mentioned it to or who is familiar with the area agrees it is a great location with very nice amenities. But it came at the cost of several additional trips to Panama I did not plan for, as well as the anxiety of making an apartment move-in ready on a forced timeline.

If we rented for a year, we would have had more time to find the bank account. We would have been able to make the apartment move-in ready with both of us being in the country instead of one of us being "boots on the ground" and the other trusting from afar....

Hopefully, you see that there is merit to starting your move on a friendly nations visa. But there are reasons why some of us choose to buy and become eligible for qualified investor visa. After having stayed in rental properties and Airbnb-type short-term rentals and just listening to the experiences of more than several expats who chose to rent, we just didn't want to deal with that situation—Furniture that is old and stained, landlords who manipulate tenants to gain entry, and the uncertainty that comes with investors who are always looking to sell your apartment. We decided to build our dream on our terms.

This is important to remember if you are buying a new apartment from a builder. Units are bare when you buy - AC (central or split units), lighting, water heater – all this is left for you to install. Labor in Panama is affordable, and if you speak Spanish, this may be the project you can manage yourself. If you do not speak Spanish, you will need an intermediary. Ask your sales agent who they know who will help you finish your project. Panama is a no-return culture. You buy it, it's yours as is. Be 100% sure that you know what you are buying, what the seller has modified, and what is or is not included. In our case, we discovered we would have three parking spaces. Now, what would happen if we only had a car?

To be prepared to buy a home in the United States, your agent will often rely on comps or comparable home sale prices. In Panama, that information is very difficult to come by – until now.

If you decide to buy a home in Panama, document your decisions here:

> **Sales agent name:**
>
> **Sales agent cell and WhatsApp:**
>
> **Handyman for make ready:**
>
> **Designer (optional):**

Criminal Background Checks and Apostille

Probably the most confusing and time-consuming process is getting your FBI report apostilled. Let's start with the requirement. For any of the visas listed above, your attorney will require a criminal background check. If you are coming from the United States, the criminal background check means the FBI report, not your local law enforcement. This is not a report from your local police department. The report you need is provided by the FBI or an FBI channeler.

The report itself is known as an Identity History Summary (IDHS). You can read more about it here https://www.fbi.gov/how-we-can-help-you/more-fbi-services-and-information/identity-history-summary-checks.

When I attempted to use the FBI directly, I was directed to a post office that would take my fingerprints. The problem? No post office within 100 miles of Austin was available. I called the FBI branch, and they Googled an answer no better than what I had. That's when I turned to a channeler, a private business that has contracted with the FBI to submit your request on your behalf. An FBI-Approved Channeler helps speed up the delivery of Identity History Summary Checks (rap sheets) on behalf of the FBI. There is a list of approved channelers, and the one I found and recommended to several people is Accurate Biometrics. Accurate Biometrics is a member of the FINRA network.

The fingerprinting is conducted at a local UPS store kiosk. The report will be emailed to you within an hour. If you don't receive it within an hour, check your junk/spam email. Do not try to access it on your phone. Wait until you are at your computer, where you can download it. It will be a PDF with a long, nondescript code as the name. To find a UPS location for fingerprinting, just register and use the zip code to locate a kiosk near you. https://accuratebiometrics.com/nationwide/services/individual/fingerprint-collection-network/#collapseOne1

Now that you have your FBI IdHS, you should get familiar with apostille. If you are not familiar, the apostille is from the Hague Convention. Effectively, it is the legal means by which countries can certify official documents as of 1961. It has a very specific format.

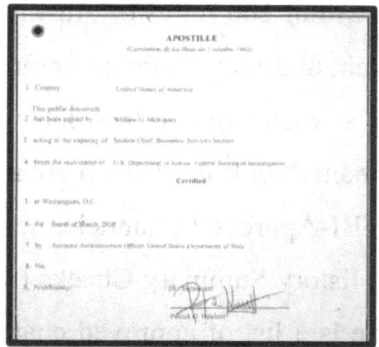

At the time of this writing, the turnaround time for having a report apostilled by the US State Department was about six weeks. There are agencies that will, for a fee, take the electronic document (PDF), have it apostilled, and return it to you via USPS with a tracking number. Otherwise, you should order paper copies of the FBI IdHS that you will manually send. I requested two copies be mailed to me. Upon evaluation, the cost to have those physical copies compared to sending the PDF to a company like apostille.net was a wash.

In Texas, the Apostille is in downtown Austin on Brazos Street. I have visited several times. They will not apostille a federal document or one from another state. Your experiences may differ.

When will you order your FBI rap sheet (IdHS)?

Where will you have your prints taken?

When did you receive your FBI rap sheet (check your junk email)?

When did you send it to be Apostilled?

When did you receive the Apostilled FBI rap sheet?

Where did you put it?

Marriage Certificate Authentication

If you are married, there are other considerations. You will need to bring your marriage certificate to your Panama attorney for immigration. It must be notarized, but the decision as to whether to authenticate or apostille is left to you.

When it came time for us to provide our marriage certificate, I decided to order a new document. I was concerned it would be modified and wanted to keep a pristine copy for our own records. So, we decided to order a notarized copy of our marriage certificate and a new birth certificate, just in case. https://www.vital-chek.com is a company that many state and county governments have outsourced to. You can check it out to see if your marriage certificate is available, and if so, it can be delivered within a couple of weeks.

Once received, we chose to have ours authenticated with the Panama Consulate located in Houston, Texas. For $30 per document, the consulate will prepare the authentication while you wait – schedule an appointment in advance. They will not see you without an appointment! Or you can mail it in along with a return envelope and postage.

The authentication will be affixed to the back of your documents and will look like this.

CONSULATE OF PANAMA
HOUSTON - TEXAS

REPÚBLICA DE PANAMÁ
MINISTERIO DE RELACIONES EXTERIORES

Departamento Consular y
Legalizaciones

**CERTIFICADO DE
AUTENTICACIÓN**

Recibo Oficial No. 1727757

Arancel No. 60

Derecho B/. $30.00

No. 1295719

El Suscrito _____ JAIME A. SOSA
NOMBRE DEL FUNCIONARIO CONSULAR
CONSUL GENERAL DE PANAMA EN HOUSTON
TÍTULO Y LUGAR DE ACREDITACIÓN

CERTIFICA:

que la firma que aparece en el documento adjunto que
dice _____ CHRIS ORMEROD _____
es **auténtica** y corresponde a la que acostumbra usar en los
documentos que autoriza en calidad de _____
JEFE DE POLICIA

Dado en la ciudad de _____ HOUSTON _____ el día _____ 8
del mes de _____ AGOSTO _____ del año _____ 2023

(SELLO)

FIRMA DEL FUNCIONARIO CONSULAR

INTERESADO

To find your local consulate, visit this page. https://www.embassyofpanama.org/consulates-of-panama-in-the-usa

Planning for Healthcare in Panama

As a US citizen, you have some of the best healthcare coverage in the world. As you consider your life in another country, you may have considered how you will pay for health care for regular outpatient visits as well as protection for unforeseen emergency hospital stays. It's important to adjust your thinking and be aware of how things operate differently in Panama. As much as possible, you should plan for your health care before making the final decision on a move.

Panama has great medical care as well, especially within Panama City. You can expect to find many United States-trained and English-speaking physicians in most facilities. There are also expat-friendly specialists like Expat Health Services that can be part of your healthcare solution. The owner, Mike Kelly, is himself an expat and has helped members of my family circle find rental properties in Panama City. But you should be aware of how things work and the decisions you will face.

Private outpatient clinics are a cost-effective solution for many Americans. For a fraction of the cost of what you pay in the United States, you can access a specialist for physical examinations and many ailments. Most are willing to come to your home and will give you their personal numbers for follow-up. Some examples of clinic networks are:

- Clinica Laboratorio Express
- Minimed
- Vitae-Health Upcare

It is not guaranteed that you will have access to English-speaking staff, but using translation services in your browser and mobile translation apps will likely help you when you need to schedule an appointment.

Hospitals are also readily accessible. You may have heard of a Johns Hopkins-affiliated hospital in the city center. While the hospitals are less expensive for similar care, they are not cheap or free. Public hospitals are available in Panama, but I would not want to be in one. After witnessing a public hospital just across the street from the cruise terminal in Colón, I have little trust that a system that would treat people most in need in these decrepit facilities would be a place that I would want to be when the time comes.

With the availability of cost-effective health care in Panama, should you carry insurance? Well, the answer here is complicated, with everyone having different perspectives. On one hand, you might be in a situation where you are able to retire and use Medicare health benefits in Panama. That's a no-brainer to take advantage of. But if you are retiring early or living the digital nomad life? Or if you simply want to protect your assets against a catastrophic health event?

We decided that we wanted to have health insurance for that last reason. We determined that it would be an acceptable expense to budget for when we looked at our family legacy of disease. What we learned is that navigating the options is difficult. For one, you really can't get a clear quote until you are a resident of Panama. You can get some estimates, and I recommend that you find and work with a health insurance broker early in your search. It may not be the top priority, but for us, it factored prominently and is a primary reason for leaving the USA.

As we started to look into our options, we thought we never got the full picture of options from any one source. This is a key point that I can't help but emphasize – business in Panama is conducted through relationships. This doesn't mean that anyone introduced to you is incompetent. Likely they are very experienced in their area. But it doesn't mean they are equipped to provide you with policies that cover:

- Local, regional, or worldwide (including or excluding USA)

- Pre-existing conditions (cancer, diabetes, lupus)

Dara and I knew that we would travel throughout the region and Europe as well as the United States. But including coverage for Colorado, New York, and Texas was an expensive policy. So, we pieced together coverage with a worldwide inpatient plan excluding the United States (we will use travel insurance when visiting) and membership with a local clinic for the first year. We will see how it goes and may drop it after the first year.

Panama brokers may not sell you this sort of policy. Panama laws impose requirements on insurance and insurance brokers that those international plans may not abide by. It doesn't mean insurance companies like Allianz are not good policies in Panama. It means you must be a much more diligent consumer as you shop a policy to get value for your dollar and only the coverage you will use.

Passports

You are very likely an international traveler. You are not new to this. If you are planning your first trip and plan to stay – I've heard of this happening exactly once – be sure that you have enough time left on your passport before it expires.

If you are planning to move to Panama using a Golden Visa, you can apply the benefits to your dependents. Sometimes, our adult children are not yet grownups – they allow things to expire as they are focused on other things of seemingly lesser importance. As of this writing, the average wait time for a passport is $10 - 13$ weeks.

If you need an expedited passport, there is a process to cut the time down from weeks to days. If you can get an appointment at a passport agency, it is possible to have a passport in your possession within two weeks and, in our case, less than a week.

https://travel.state.gov/content/travel/en/passports/get-fast/passport-agencies.html

Transporting Your Pet

For many pet owners, how to get your fur baby from the US to Panama is a particular challenge. Panama, like other countries, has specific rules to follow when bringing a pet. Airlines also have placed embargos on transporting pets in cargo, especially during hot summer months. Some will allow you to bring pets into the cabin, while others do not. We expect airlines to continue to make policy changes with regard to pets, so you should check with your carrier as far as 60 days out from your goal date.

To bring your pet to Panama has some requirements that you can find on the Panama Embassy website: https://www.embassy-ofpanama.org/travelling-with-pets-1. In summary, you should be prepared to:

1. Provide proof of vaccinations, especially rabies. Panama will want a signed certificate with the date, manufacturer, and lot number of the vaccine.

2. Be sure your pet has a microchip.

3. A USDA Certificate of Good Health must be completed within ten days of travel. The certificate must be authenti-cated (the apostille requirement has been waived for a couple of years). https://www.aphis.usda.gov/aphis/pet-travel/by-country/pettravel-panama

4.   A home quarantine request must also be completed.

It's also important to note that you should arrive during the business hours of PTY; otherwise, your pet could be kept overnight, unable to clear customs. This would be even worse for a late Friday arrival. So, plan your travel for Monday through Thursday.

Having covered the country requirements, below are the most common transport options that we came across with regard to our four-year-old labradoodle, Luna.

- Bring the dog into the cabin as a personal item.

- Bring the dog as a service or support dog.

- Call American Airlines for transporting as a support dog +1 (800) 433-7300

- Call Copa Airlines for transporting as a service dog +1 (786) 840-COPA (2672)

- Call Delta Airlines for transporting as a service dog +1 (404) 309-3434

- Call United Airlines for transporting as a service dog +1 (800) 228-2744

- Contact the airline carrier for transport in the cargo area.

- American Airlines Cargo PetEmbark program details are found here https://www.aacargo.com/learn/animals.html

- Copa Airlines Cargo pet service details are here
  https://www.copacargo.com/html/user/default.aspx?pageid=13&lang=en

- Delta Airlines currently has an embargo in place for international flights. See information here
  https://www.delta.com/us/en/pet-travel/international-connection-pet-travel

- United Airlines PetSafe program has been suspended. You can find current information here
  https://www.united.com/en/us/fly/travel/traveling-with-pets.html

- Work with a pet transport company. Some airlines will only work with pet transport companies that are International Pet and Animal Transportation Association (IPATA) member-certified. IPATA maintains a list of shippers
  https://www.ipata.org/find-ipata-pet-shippers. The shortlist can be found below:

- Canal Movers Logistics Corp.

- Panama Pet Relocation / Planet Pet Relocation

- Pets Go Global

One of the better-organized sites for transporting a pet is airlinespet.com https://airlinespet.com/. Trisha does a great job of providing useful information on airline policy, scams, and travel crates. Though not specific to international travel to Panama, it's a great resource for understanding airline policies.

Among the expat community, PetsGoGlobal stands out as a frequently endorsed choice. I've received several positive reviews about their services, but there's a hitch: their list of departure airports is quite restricted. To give an example, our journey with Luna required us to drive from Texas to Florida to catch a flight from Miami International Airport. After weighing our options, we partnered with PetsGoGlobal, and our experience with Ms. Marla Paul was absolutely commendable. They're recognized for their stellar reputation, and even if it meant paying a premium, the convenience they offered was well worth it.

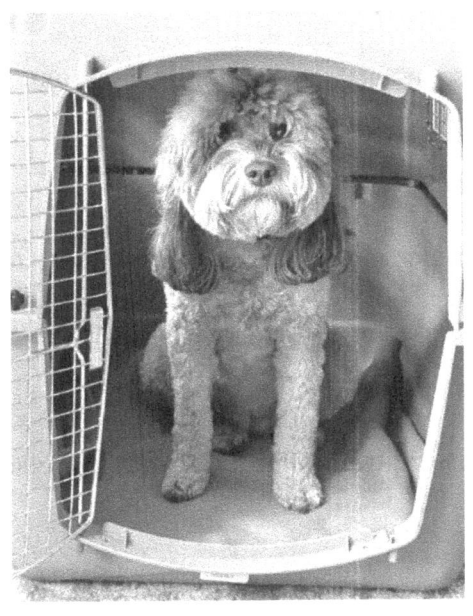

Your Project Plan

Moving internationally is a complex process, and proper sequencing of tasks can make the transition smoother. Here's a suggested sequence, along with an estimated time frame for each action:

1. **Understand the visa options** (1-2 weeks)

- Research online, read expat forums and reach out to the Panamanian consulate.

2. **Find a Panama lawyer specializing in visa** (2-3 weeks)

- Seek referrals, read reviews, and schedule initial consultations.

3. **Get your FBI report apostilled** (4-6 weeks)

- This process includes obtaining the report and then having it apostilled. The apostille process can vary in time, so it's best to start early.

4. **Get your marriage certificate authenticated** (2-4 weeks)

- If you're married and your spouse is also moving, this step is vital for visa purposes.

5. **Move to international bank account** (2-3 weeks)

- Start by researching banks that offer international benefits like waiving transaction fees and wire transfers. Open an account and start transitioning funds.

6. **Find a Panama local bank to join** (3-4 weeks)

- This will be easier once you're in the country, but you can start your research ahead of time. Ask your lawyer to make introductions on your behalf.

7. **Downsize home in the United States to prepare to move** (6-12 weeks)

- Begin by decluttering, selling, donating, or storing items. Depending on the size of your home and how much you own, this can be a time-consuming step.

8. **Locate a rental or home to purchase** (4-8 weeks)

- You can start your research online, but you might want to finalize this once you're in Panama. It's beneficial to see properties in person.

9. **Make a plan to move your pet if necessary** (4-6 weeks)

- This includes researching pet relocation services, ensuring your pet meets Panama's import requirements, and getting any necessary vaccinations or health certificates.

Total Time: Roughly 6-7 months (28-40 weeks).

Let's put it all together.

Task	Page	Notes	Date	Months until
#	#		Goal date minus weeks	Months until
1	*4*	*Arrival date to our new home*	*November 5, 2024*	*12 months*
2	*17*	*Renew our passports*	*March 5, 2024*	*4 months*

There are different methods to manage a project. Some people like the traditional project management tools and Gantt charts. Others prefer checklists. My wife and I use Kanban boards. We start a project with one of those giant post-it notes you can get from Office Depot or Staples. We put three columns: To do, In Process, Done. We have the small post-it notes with tasks, owners, and due dates that we move across. This means we both have all the information necessary at a glance. The truth is that the best project management tool is the one that works best for the people expected to participate and complete the tasks.

Conclusion

We hope this workbook has been useful for you. I want to thank my fellow expats, relocation consultants, real estate sales agents, and rental agents for their support. When in doubt, they are your best source of information for Panama. The goal of this workbook is to help you in the preparation before you are in their care.

If you've got to the end and have questions, let's talk. You can schedule 30 minutes with me using the link below:

https://calendly.com/leap_with_aaron/30min

We look forward to meeting you and helping you reach your goals.